YOU ARE HOME

Affirmations to Lighten Your Heart & Lift Your Soul

Tarn Ellis

MANDALA

SAN RAFAEL LOS ANGELES LONDON

YOU ARE HOME

was written to inspire and heal you.

This book is a love letter to your soul.
It empowers you to step into your full potential.
To follow your intuition and listen to your heart.
To work your magic. To bloom.

You Are Home reminds you of your worth and purpose.
You may seek both reassurance and encouragement here.
And you will find yourself uplifted, energized, and affirmed.

The women in these pages are drawn without faces
so that you can attach your own meaning to them.
Interpret each image in whatever way speaks most deeply to you.
Meditate on how the art makes you feel.

This book is a mirror. You will see yourself reflected in it.

So let *You Are Home*
take you on a journey of self-love.

HOW TO USE THIS BOOK

You Are Home can be read cover to cover.
But it can also be used to inspire you.
Flip to any page to bring wisdom and color to your day.
Display it on an altar, open to your favorite affirmation.
Or set it on your coffee table or nightstand for casual perusal.

This book is all about you.
There is no right or wrong way to soak in its insights.

THEMES

THE LITTLE THINGS: Practicing gratitude.

UNIVERSAL CONNECTION: Finding comfort in community.

LESSONS IN LOVE: Opening your heart to meaningful relationships.

NOTES ON NATURE: Receiving the wisdom of the natural world.

ACCEPTANCE: Allowing things to be as they are.

SELF-CARE: Cultivating peace from within.

MANIFESTING DREAMS: Creating the life you want.

THE LITTLE THINGS

It's the little things
that make up your life.
The simple pleasures.
The details that almost
escape your notice.

But pay attention.
There is an enormous
amount of joy to be
found within them.

In the end, the little things
are actually the big things.

And picnics in the grass on a long summer's day.

Simple pleasure:
finishing a good book.

And the joy and privilege of being able to learn. There is so much knowledge at our fingertips.

Simple pleasure:
the sun's warmth
on your skin
after a long, cold winter.

And the smell and feel
of freshly washed sheets.
Laundry, waving in the wind,
casting shadows. A washing line,
and all the life it alludes to.

Simple pleasure:

waking up S L O W L Y.

Sip your morning coffee or tea
with great appreciation
for this new day that
you have been blessed with.

It takes very little to live a happy life.

Once your basic needs are met, the less you want, the easier it will be to feel content.

Start practicing
gratitude.

Say thank you for everything, no matter how small.

Happiness is
everywhere.

It's in your ability
to appreciate
the little things.

In the petal
of a flower.

In the ground
beneath you.

In the stillness you feel when you're alone.

In the gratitude for your present circumstances.

In your heart.

Count your blessings.

There is so much to be grateful for.

When we need a little less, we will stop yearning for more.

Eventually, meeting our basic needs will be enough to feel complete.

We can feel satisfied just lying in the overgrown grass,
reading an old book, flowers tickling our bare feet.

And we will understand that
that is all we really need.

UNIVERSAL CONNECTION

Sitting under a night sky
brimming with stars,
you might find
yourself feeling small.
But it should
fill you with comfort,
knowing that every other
human on Earth
is just like you.
Small, but integral.

We are interconnected.

The trees, the fish, the moon, the stars, the plants, the air.

We are a part of it all.

Invisible tendrils of spirit and magic link us together.

You are within everything,
and everything is within you.
We are all children of the universe.

May we come together in love and acceptance,
knowing we all have the right to be here.

We are
all equal.

Healthy connections
are deeply healing.

There is room for all of us to bloom
in this world of abundance.

Isn't it beautiful

that we are all experiencing

different versions of the same truth?

Dance together.

After all, we're dancing under the same sky.

The universe weaves circles of magic around us.

Connecting us.
Uniting us.
Reminding us.

We are not alone.

Above all else,
we must not lose our sense
of awe and wonder.

The entire
universe
is inside you.

It may be true that we are all different.
We are each unique, living distinct lives.
But in the grand scheme of the universe,
we are all experiencing this miraculous thing called life.

LESSONS IN LOVE

You may have
spent a lot of time
looking for love
in the wrong places.

Connection, romance,
and intimacy are only attainable
when you learn this simple truth:
Love comes from within.

Love is our very essence.

When you strip everything else away—
thoughts, perception, ego—
you will discover that
you are made of pure love.

She walked alone, over countless mountains,

through endless valleys, losing count of the sunsets,

At the crossroads, she stopped.

"Which way?" she asked.

"Follow your heart," whispered the wind.

LOVE IS INFINITE

In one way, you love your family. In another way,
you love your friends. In another way, you love
your partner. In another way, you love a stranger.
In another way, you love the universe.
And in another way . . . you love yourself.

If you love someone,
let them know.

Remind yourself
that all of the love
is already within you.

It never leaves.

It resides within
your heart.

Make deep connections, not deep attachments.

No matter what, you are
worthy of love.
Stop waiting around for someone to
bring you flowers. Give them to yourself.
Take yourself on dates.
Life is romantic,
even when you're alone.

NOTES ON TENDERHEARTEDNESS

Be soft.

Cry whenever
you feel like it.

As much as you can help it,
do not allow time
to harden you.

Keep your heart open,
no matter how many times
it breaks. Its ability to heal
will surprise you.

Be gentle.

Vulnerability is not
your weakness.
It's your power.

Be kind to yourself
as well as others.

These mountains don't seem quite so steep
when we climb them together.

When it's a question of head or heart,
always choose your heart.

The head plays it safe,
considering the past
to calculate the future.

The heart, on the other hand,
takes risks. It lives in the present.
It may lead you into danger,
but this is where you can
nourish your being,
reach your potential, grow.

You can never go astray,
listening to your heart.

You will never feel divided.

You will always be aligned
with your true purpose.

NOTES ON NATURE

Spend time in the living, breathing
world that surrounds you.
Feel its awesome presence.
Open yourself up
to receive its wisdom.

Nature is whispering its secrets.
All we have to do
is quiet our minds and listen.

The Earth speaks to all of us.

Notice the quietly confident plants.

Never hurried, never worried.

Just knowing, just growing,

Just being.

Take inspiration.

Simply exist.

There is nothing
more to be done.

Nourish yourself
with water,
sunlight, rest,
fresh air, space.
As if you are
a little seedling,
growing into
the mightiest oak.

Just like the humble seedling,
you contain infinite potential.

We live in a universe of
infinitely repeating patterns.
If you look closely,
you'll see the patterns
in your own life as well.

Consider the cyclical nature of life.
The way the phases come and go and come again.
You can learn from them, and use them as a tool for growth.
You will come to understand that no matter
which phase you're passing through,
eventually you will be whole again.

You are wild and free.

Your soul sings the same song as the earth beneath you.

As the plants around you.

As the sun and moon above you.

Be in your wild.

Your life is like a garden.

Water it. Let the birds visit. Take time to smell the flowers.

Sometimes, weeds will grow. You might need to uproot them.

But leave the wildflowers. Not everything has to be planned.

Let go of perfection.

Your garden doesn't have to

be neat for it to be beautiful.

But sometimes it's
not about the garden.

It's about going deep into the forest
alone and staying there until you feel
at one with the trees.

Leave the beaten track. Get lost.
Be open to whatever you might find,
or the possibility of not finding
anything at all.

Just listen to the whisper
of the woods..

Your life is also like a river.
Ride the current with confidence.
Appreciate its meandering path
and gentle bends. Feel weightless.
Go with the flow.

When the water grows turbulent,
as you fight to keep your head above,
learn what you can from the struggle.

Your destination may be uncertain,
but you must trust the river
and its ever-changing course.

The dreary days are necessary.
You need rain to grow.

Be grounded.

Be barefoot and free.

Feel the earth beneath you.

Let the pure energy
of the soil flow into
and through you.

Sit in nature. Walk barefoot.
Pay close attention to the vibrations from the Earth.

In these moments,
you are totally conscious,
completely awake,
fully aware that you are
one with creation.

If you have a question
to which you don't know the answer,
you can always ask the trees.

We are guests on this planet.

Tread lightly.

Look after our home.

Look after our mother.

Live a life that
respects the planet.

Be a guardian, a protector.
Leave only footprints.

Make your time here
a love letter to the earth.

As we heal the Earth, the Earth heals us.

ACCEPTANCE

Fighting the flow of life
isn't fruitful.

People, possessions,
youth, even emotions . . .
everything comes and goes.
In the end,
nothing is ours to keep.

Accepting the course of life
without judgment or attachment
brings an incredible amount of peace.

Your thoughts and feelings
are always valid.

Just remember that
they're not always true.

She saw her life from a new perspective.

Maybe it was her seat at the peak of a tall mountain.
Or maybe it was the ravens soaring on the breeze below.

But she realized that everything she was
existed only in that moment.

Before, she was different.
Later, she would become something new.

But for now,
she was just a girl watching the sunset.
And that was enough.

When loneliness comes, sit with it. Discover what's on the other side.

Aloneness will light your path, and introspection
will let you get to know your true self.

Through solitude, you will learn
that you are enough.

Find the
peace
in your
solitude.

You are brave,
even if you don't feel fearless.
You are still here, showing up,
despite all the challenges
you have faced.
And that is a triumph.

Mindfulness means paying attention to the present moment, without judgment.

Can you be here now, without wishing things were different? Or hoping things won't change?

Can you stay present, without drifting into the past or imagined future, long enough to feel this moment for what it truly is?

Sometimes you might get lost in a wave of thought or emotion and lose sight of the shore.

But remember, you are not the waves.

You are the ocean.

Drop out of your head
and into your body.

If you feel sorrow,
try to view it
with new eyes.

Yes, it is yours.
But it is not
yours to keep.

Try to accept every emotion without judgment.
Emotions are neither good nor bad.

They are simply part of our
authentic experience.

All the thoughts in your head

that no longer serve you . . .

Just let them float by.

Free yourself from the illusion of the "good old days."
Stop living for the future. There is only here and now.
Accept every moment for what it is.

Nothing is permanent.
Tomorrow is not promised.

If you can accept that
change is inevitable,
you will set yourself free.

When you feel a little lost,
when you're not exactly sure
what you're doing here,
or how you got here,
or where to go next,
just remember . . .

You are exactly
where you need to be.

Although you may travel far and wide,
remember that no matter where you find yourself,

You are home.

SELF-CARE

Learn the importance
of taking care of yourself.
Show yourself
the same love,
compassion, and kindness
that you show others.
The greatest gift
you have to offer
is being wholly and
unapologetically yourself.

Even when the chaos of life
feels like it might just
swallow you whole,
you always have
the ability to stop.

Slow down.

Peace and serenity are within your grasp.
No matter how loud the world around you gets,
you can always return home to yourself.

Sit quietly.

Go inward.

Cultivate an oasis
within yourself.

Try your best not to take things personally.

How other people treat you is a reflection of themselves.

When you overcome the resistance and fear
and allow yourself to grow,
you will soon see just how
extraordinary you can be.

Be in the mystery
of who you are.

Self-love isn't selfish. It's essential.

You have a greater capacity to take care of others when you take care of yourself first.

When you feel empty,
drink from your well.

Don't concern yourself
with perfection.

You are already perfect.

You cannot possibly
be anything less.

So put your ideas, your work,
your self out there.

Your power lies in your intricacies.
In what sets you apart.

Let go of your guilt.
You don't have to carry
it with you anymore.

You can say, "I'm sorry,"
but don't wait for
anyone's forgiveness.

You must forgive yourself
to find your peace.

When you consider your inner child,
you have an even greater capacity
to be gentle with yourself.

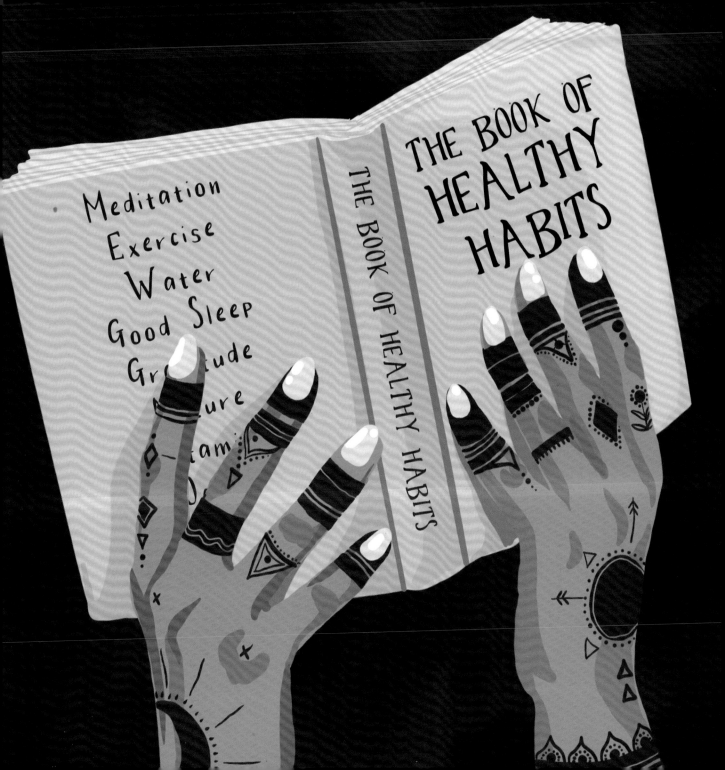

You are capable of everything you set your mind to.

Remember,
your worth is
not measured
by your
productivity.

Do your best,
then take rest.

Let go of the day. Know that you have done enough. You deserve to rest, recharge, repair. Everything else can wait.
Breathe Deep
Hot
Cold

MANIFESTING DREAMS

Despite all of the things
that are out of your control,
you are still in charge
of your own life.
You are an artist,
and you are here to
create the most beautiful
artwork on your canvas.
Your dreams are big,
and your heart is open.

Everything you do
reflects back to you.

All of your thoughts and actions,
even the ones that go unnoticed,
are powerful.

You are magnetic.

So be grateful. Be thankful.
Be prepared to receive blessings.

Don't be afraid to ask for what you want,
or for guidance, or for change.

Your life can be magnificent,
if you allow it to be.

The universe is always listening.

Give what you want to receive.

KINDNESS

COMPASSION

UNDERSTANDING

GRACE

PEACE

LOVE

You are not the same person from one day to the next.

You are multifaceted, always changing and evolving.

You can choose to be whoever you want.

You can wake up and think,

"Today I will be a musician!"

"Or a florist!"

"Or a gardener!"

The point is . . .

You are
limitless.

You can be
anything
you want to be.

Have no fear.

Whatever is meant for you will not pass you by.

Abundance is a mindset.

Stop living in fear or competition.
Believe, with your whole heart,
that there is enough for everyone.

And with that belief, you will invite
a greater bounty into your life.

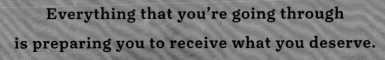

Everything that you're going through

is preparing you to receive what you deserve.

You can choose
to turn the page
whenever it feels right.

You can close the chapter,
or the whole book.

Have no fear.
A new one awaits.

Get out and see the world.

Wanderlust is the heart's way of telling us
not to close ourselves off to possibilities.

Embrace uncertainty.

Don't let fear of the unknown
dictate your road.
Your best life could be waiting
just beyond your comfort zone.

You get to decide
what you carry with you.

Create a life you don't feel
the need to escape from.

Your life is always speaking to you.
Sometimes there is a whisper deep within,
nudging you in the right direction.

It says,
"This way!
Follow me!"
Listen carefully.

Other times it's a
feeling in the pit
of your stomach.
Or a shiver
running down
your spine.
Or the hairs
rising on the back
of your neck.

Whatever it is,
don't ignore it.

We are sometimes afraid to listen
to this deep inner stirring,
because it tells us where we are out
of alignment with ourselves.

It tells us we need to change something.

But have no fear. Change is growth.

When you realize that you are an artist . . .

and that your life is a blank canvas ready for you to paint whatever you desire . . .

you start to dream bigger.

Dare to dream.

Your canvas is limitless.
You are limitless.

What could you manifest
if you knew that no dream
was too big?

Believe in the future you are creating . . .

with all of your heart.

Open yourself up
to all possibilities.

There is incredible magic
in the unknown.

SOONER OR LATER, YOU'LL KNOW IT'S TIME TO START SOMETHING NEW.

AND IT WILL BE MAGIC.

ABOUT THE AUTHOR

Tarn Ellis is an artist and writer from the south of England. She is best known for her faceless style and her diverse and inclusive depictions of women. Tarn takes inspiration from nature, the ocean, and yogic philosophy, transporting her audience to dreamlike worlds. With a background in psychology and mindfulness, she creates thought-provoking illustrations paired with words of love and acceptance. She hopes to uplift and inspire her audience to live more authentic, adventurous, and carefree lives, following their passions and embracing their unique journeys.

MANDALA

An imprint of MandalaEarth
PO Box 3088
San Rafael, CA 94912
www.MandalaEarth.com

 Find us on Facebook: www.facebook.com/MandalaEarth
Follow us on Twitter: @MandalaEarth

Publisher Raoul Goff
Associate Publisher Roger Shaw
Publishing Director Katie Killebrew
Editorial Assistant Amanda Nelson
Editor Peter Adrian Behravesh
VP, Creative Director Chrissy Kwasnik
Art Director Ashley Quackenbush
Senior Designer Stephanie Odeh
VP Manufacturing Alix Nicholaeff
Senior Production Manager Joshua Smith
Senior Production Manager, Subsidiary Rights Lina s Palma-Temena

ISBN: 979-8-88762-092-3

Manufactured in China by Insight Editions
10 9 8 7 6 5 4 3 2 1

Insight Editions, in association with Roots of Peace, will plant two trees for each tree used in the manufacturing of this book. Roots of Peace is an internationally renowned humanitarian organization dedicated to eradicating land mines worldwide and converting war-torn lands into productive farms and wildlife habitats. Roots of Peace will plant two million fruit and nut trees in Afghanistan and provide farmers there with the skills and support necessary for sustainable land use.